I'M ~~NOT~~ ENOUGH

Journal

© 2022 Leanne Whitfield, First Edition

All rights reserved. No portion of this book may be reproduced, stored in a retrieval system, or transmitted in any form or by any means – electronic, mechanical, photocopy, recording, scanning or other – except for brief quotations in critical reviews or articles, without the prior written permission of the publisher.

Published in Perth Western Australia by Refiners Fire Publishing® PTY LTD.

Scripture quotations are taken from the Holy Bible, New Living Translation, copyright © 1996, 2004, 2015 by Tyndale House Foundation. Used by permission of Tyndale House Publishers, Inc., Carol Stream, Illinois 60188. All rights reserved.

Any internet addresses, phone numbers, or company or product information printed in this book are offered as a resource and are not intended in any way to be or to imply an endorsement by Refiners Fire Publishing®, nor does Refiners Fire Publishing® vouch for the existence, content, or services of these sites, phone numbers, companies, or products beyond the life of this book.

ISBN-13: 978-0-6485832-5-7 (Soft Cover)

Cover design: Glenn and Leanne Whitfield
Interior Design: Glenn and Leanne Whitfield

Printed in Australia

Welcome to the

I'm Enough Journal!

If we want to get serious about realising our worth and value it is going to take some work. The great news is that we don't have to do it alone, we have the Holy Spirit to help us navigate.

This journal is an opportunity for you to spend time with God and record your journey into freedom. There is plenty of room to journal and room to record your responses to the questions I asked at the end of chapters 7 through to 12. Which ever way you approach it, this is your opportunity for reflection and revelation in the area of value and worth.

Remember, it is for Freedom Christ has set us free, so let's no longer be enslaved to the lie of not being enough.

Take your time, value this journey because it may just change your life!

"I praise you because I am fearfully and wonderfully made"

Psalm 139:14

The key to freedom from feeling "not enough" is moving away from trying to be accepted to knowing that you are accepted by God

I'm Enough: Chapter 7

God showed His great love for us by sending Christ to die for us while we were still sinners

Romans 5:8

When we allow God to heal us, we no longer have to manage our pain and we get to enjoy the freedom of being released

I'm Enough: Chapter 8

God raised us up with Christ and seated us with Him in the heavenly realms in Christ Jesus

Ephesians 2:6

God is not looking at our accolades, He's looking for willing hearts

I'm Enough: Chapter 9

"For I know the plans I have for you," declares the Lord, "plans to prosper you and not to harm you, plans to give you hope and a future"

Jeremiah 29:11

Healthy life-giving thoughts are aligned with the word of God and what He says about us

I'm Enough: Chapter 10

So God created man in His own image, in the image of God He created him; male and female He created them

Genesis 1:27

Knowing your worth and value in Christ is the absolute key to breaking free from a world of "I'm not enough"

I'm Enough: Chapter 11

See what kind of love the Father has given to us, that we should be called children of God

1 John 3:1

Don't stay in the past, look forward and then you'll move forward

I'm Enough: Chapter 12

www.ingramcontent.com/pod-product-compliance
Lightning Source LLC
Chambersburg PA
CBHW051539010526
44107CB00064B/2786